Copyright © 2022 by O C. Mogounn

All rights reserved.

No part of this publication may be reproduced, distributed, or transmitted in any form or by any means, including photocopying, recording, or other electronic or mechanical methods, without prior written permission of the publisher, except in case of brief quotations embodied in reviews and certain other non-commercial uses permitted by copyright law.

First edition August 2022

Book Editing by ......Stacey Grammargal
Cover design by ....O C. Mogounn

ISBN: 978-1-7782423-0-4 (Paperback)
ISBN: 978-1-7782423-2-8 (Ebook)
ISBN: 978-1-7782423-1-1 (Hardcover)

52	EMPRESS MARIE CLAIRE BOHNEUR Haiti	72	SEH-DONG-HONG-BEH Benin
54	QUEEN OF SHEBA, MAKEDA Ethiopia	74	DAHOMEY AMAZONS Benin
56	PRINCESS AQUALTUNE Congo	76	QUEEN HATSHEPSUT Egypt
58	PRIESTESS KIMPA VITA Congo	78	QUEEN YAA ASANTEWAA Ghana
60	EMPRESS TAYTU Ethiopia	82	QUEEN MWANA MKISI Kenya
62	QUEEN NDATE YALLA Senegal	84	METE LELE GEORGETTE Cameroon
64	QUEEN DIHYA Algeria	88	TOMORROW'S TRAILBLAZERS
66	QUEEN CALIFIA California Island	90	FURTHER READING
68	QUEEN CLEOPATRA Egypt	91	ACKNOWLEDGMENTS
70	RAIN QUEENS OF SOUTH AFRICA South Africa	92	ABOUT THE AUTHOR

PREFACE

There are many reasons why this book needed to be written. One of them is the trust and encouragement we received from our Kickstarter backers all over the world, not to mention the friends and family who supported this project from the start.

Growing up as a child, I never heard tales of black African heroes. This indeed left a huge gap within me. Relying more on Western characters, I found myself losing some self-esteem over time because the truth is, representation is important. Every child deserves to have a hero, a princess, a fairy godmother that looks like them.

This is how everything took off. One ordinary day, I went grocery shopping at Walmart. Being a mom of two beautiful girls and a boy, I always look around whenever I stumble on cute clothes. This is how I happened to desert the food section and found myself browsing through the cute Disney princess T-shirt dresses found on the clothing racks. Something struck me as I went through the clothes: though extremely beautiful, none of the cute Disney princess drawings looked like any of my girls. Coming back home, I told myself, "I wish I could find girls' clothes with cute drawings of beautiful black princesses." Then immediately as the thought left me, I asked myself, "Why not create them?"

This is how the project of Barbuzaar came about. But before I could introduce to the world fictional African princesses and queens, I felt like it was my responsibility to shine light on Africa's true ancient princesses and queens. How shocked I was when I was going through the research and discovered the wealth of information I stumbled upon—wonderful stories and legends of real heroes that have never been explored. Cutting it short, going through this project was a real

Don't forget to sign up for our monthly newsletter and follow us on Instagram.

So you won't miss out on great reads, special offers, giveaways, updates from the author, and our upcoming African-inspired fairy-tale series

@Barbuzaar

Contents

6 — PREFACE	**30** — QUEEN YODIT GUDIT / Ethiopia
8 — QUEEN NJINGA / Angola	**32** — QUEEN MUHUMUZA / Rwanda
12 — QUEEN ARRAWELO / Eritrea	**34** — PRINCESS YENNENGA / Burkina Faso
14 — QUEEN AMINA / Nigeria	**38** — QUEEN NANDI / South Africa
18 — QUEEN NANNY / Jamaica	**40** — QUEEN AMINERENAS / Sudan
20 — QUEEN MOREMI / Nigeria	**42** — PRINCESS MKABAYI / South Africa
24 — QUEEN ABLA POKOU / Ghana	**46** — QUEEN RANAVALONA / Madagascar
26 — QUEEN IDIA / Benin	**48** — QUEEN NEFERTITI / Egypt
28 — QUEEN LILIUOKALANI / Hawaii	**50** — PRIESTESS NEHANDA / Zimbabwe

PREFACE

delight of wonderful discoveries, and I hope you enjoy every bit of these stories as much as I did.

Discover the real African princesses and queens. The true heroes!
—O C. Mogounn

QUEEN NJINGA

(1583 – 1663)

Once upon a time, there lived a little girl called Njinga. She was the daughter of King Kilombo. Her name, Njinga, meaning "to twist or to turn," was given to her after she came out of her mother's womb with the umbilical cord wrapped around her neck. This was said to indicate that the child would grow up to be a powerful person. Njinga had three siblings: two sisters and a brother. She was a brilliant and fearless child and was her father's favorite. Growing up, the princess was taught to read and write and was trained as a warrior to battle alongside her brothers.

Njinga was always by her father's side, and he took her with him whenever he wanted to perform his official duties. As a result, she learned a lot around him, which she would eventually use in the future. From the moment the Portuguese visited the Ndongo people in 1575, they did everything possible to take over their land. King Kilombo tried hard to defend his people, but none of his tactics worked. At the king's death, Njinga's brother Mbandi ascended the throne. Mbandi had always been jealous of his sister Njinga, and once he became king, he did everything to ensure that she never turned against him.

Fearing for her life, Njinga ran away into a neighboring kingdom called Matamba after a series of cruel mistreatment from her brother. Unable to properly stand against the Portuguese, King Mbandi was expelled from his court, and, in despair, he asked his sister to assist him by acting as his emissary to the Portuguese in Luanda. For the sake of her people, she agreed to the diplomatic mission. Njinga arrived in Luanda at the head of a massive delegation. She was carried by her servants and dressed in luxurious traditional Ndongo apparel, even though Ndongo leaders were

ILLUSTRATED BY
BABA AMINU MUSTAPHA

expected to meet with the Portuguese in Western clothing. She did this intentionally to demonstrate to them that the Ndongos' traditional attire was not inferior to theirs. The Portuguese all sat on chairs as she walked into the meeting. Njinga noticed no chair had been reserved for her. Only a mat had been placed on the floor, on which they expected her to kneel. This type of practice was commonly used by the Portuguese to display their supremacy. Noble Njinga refused to be belittled, and instead, at her command, one of her servants got down on all fours on the mat and acted as her chair.

She was a skilled and tenacious negotiator. At the end of the meeting, she agreed on the terms of a peace treaty with the governor. After this, Njinga came home triumphant and glorified. Disgraced, King Mbandi committed suicide. After his death, Njinga took control of Ndongo, though many opposed her because she was a woman. Thanks to her excellent leadership, she challenged the Portuguese dominance of her kingdom and declared her kingdom a free state.

The Portuguese later realized they could not intimidate this dignified warrior queen or bend her to their will so easily. As a result, they switched tactics, claiming she was not suited to ruling because she was a woman and needed to be replaced. When Queen Njinga heard that officials in Luanda had decided to capture her, she fled with her supporters to the Matamba region, where she gathered new allies and created an entirely new government. She then used her army to block Portuguese influence in the region, literally leading her army into battle all by herself.

Queen Njinga would spend forty years fighting against the Portuguese, using her intelligent military tactics to keep them away. Later, she was officially recognized as the ruler of the Ndongo and Matamba. The Portuguese were unable to gain a stronghold in her territory while she was on the throne. She wore a royal crown whenever she performed formal tasks and always dressed gorgeously in the style of her ancestors.

Queen Njinga paved the way for women to be in positions of leadership. She is held up as a symbol of freedom and resistance to oppression and is celebrated as the mother of modern-day Angola.

QUEEN ARRAWEELO

(UNKNOWN)

Once upon a time, there was a kingdom in modern-day Somalia governed by a powerful and beautiful queen. Ebla Awad was the queen's name, but everyone called her "Queen Arraweelo." She was the firstborn of a family of three girls and the natural heir to the throne. Once Arraweelo was crowned queen, she became a figure of female empowerment.

During her rule, her husband objected to her self-proclaimed role as the provider for the entire society. He firmly believed that women should only focus on domestic responsibilities and leave every other matter to men. Arraweelo rebelled against her husband and demanded that all women in the country abandon their womanly roles. The strike was successful, and men eventually took on additional child-rearing responsibilities, thereby creating a role reversal in the kingdom.

Queen Arraweelo thought this role switching was necessary since she saw women as natural peacekeepers. As a child, she realized that women were not treated fairly and that men were most frequently the instigators, participants, and conductors of war and politics. The queen fought not just for women's liberation but also for women's leadership, as she considered women better and more efficient leaders. With her all-female army, she led an all-women's rebellion in which she overthrew many kings.

Arraweelo's tale continues to inspire Somalian girls and women. She is regarded as a symbol of bravery and perseverance. Today, the most confident and bold girls in Somalia are nicknamed Arraweelo.

ILLUSTRATED BY
Taiye Okoh

QUEEN AMINA

(1533 - 1610)

Once upon a time, there was a little girl named Amina. She was the daughter of King Nikatau and Queen Bakwa of Turunku. From a very young age, Amina's leadership abilities were recognized by her grandfather. He allowed her to attend state meetings and provided her with all the necessary knowledge she needed to become a great leader. Following the death of her parents, Amina's brother Karama ascended to the throne of Zazzau. Amina had already distinguished herself as a leading warrior in her brother's troops and had also gathered recognition for her military abilities. After her brother died, it was no surprise that she became queen of Zazzau.

Queen Amina launched a military attack against her neighbor to expand Zazzau territory only three months after her coronation. Though she was considered inferior as a ruler because she was a woman, she surprisingly surpassed all expectations. Queen Amina removed all obstacles to her nation's direct access to the Atlantic Coast, allowing them to trade safely. To do so, she personally commanded military operations of over twenty thousand men and one hundred well-trained cavalry troops in many battles.

Queen Amina conquered vast lands. Under her rule, Zazzau controlled more territory than ever before. She created trade routes throughout Northern Africa, her kingdom was the most extensive amongst the Hausa kingdoms, and she brought unheard-of wealth to the land and boosted her kingdom's wealth with gold, slaves, and new crops. Her troops used metal armor in battle, including iron helmets and chain mail, as her people were talented metal workers.

ILLUSTRATED BY
BABA AMINU MUSTAPHA

Queen Amina is also credited with designing the city's formidable earthen walls, which formed the model for defenses used by all Hausa states. Many of these fortifications, known as ganuwar Amina or Amina's walls, were built around the various cities she conquered.

To this date, these walls have stood as a lasting testament to her triumphant reign. Though she had a great number of suitors at an early age, she refused to marry, fearing she might lose her power if she did so. As a result, she did not have a family of her own and died after thirty-four years of glorious reign. Everything Amina did as a queen exceeded what her male predecessors had done. She continues to represent the spirit of womanhood's strength.

Today, Queen Amina is also celebrated in traditional Hausa praise songs as "Amina, daughter of Nikatau, a woman as capable as a man."

WHO IS YOUR ROLE MODEL AND WHY?

QUEEN NANNY
(1686-1733)

Hundreds of years ago, a courageous warrior queen lived in the mountains of Jamaica. She taught her people how to survive, battle, and obtain freedom. She was the leader of the Maroons. Maroons were slaves who escaped and established autonomous settlements.

Nanny herself was an escaped slave. She and her four brothers were able to escape from their plantations to the highlands and jungles, where they established Nanny Town, a village in the mountains that was difficult to attack. Nanny was an expert in guerrilla tactics. She trained her people on how to strategically infiltrate the British operations. Her warriors invaded plantations, burning them down and taking with them arms, food, and captives who were released on the condition that they join the Maroons.

Nanny carried out several successful raids to free slaves held on plantations. Under her command, more than one thousand slaves were successfully rescued from sugarcane plantations across the colony. She built fortified defenses around many impenetrable communities. She was the leader of a self-sustaining settlement that produced music, and art and maintained the people's traditional customs. Thanks to Nanny's great leadership, Nanny Town and the Maroons prospered and multiplied. The triumph of the Maroons humiliated and threatened the British colonial authorities.

The Maroons were unstoppable. In the end, Nanny negotiated a profitable peace treaty to end the conflict. Today, her face is on the country's $500 bill, and thanks to her bravery, Nanny Town, now known as Moore Town, remains an autonomous region under the self-government of the Maroon people.

ILLUSTRATED BY
TAIYE OKOH

QUEEN MOREMI
(20TH CENTURY)

A very long time ago, in the ancient town of Ile-Ife, there lived a woman named Moremi. In the entire Yoruba city-state, there was not anyone as beautiful as her. Moremi was not only incredibly beautiful, but also she was courageous and wise. The people of Ile-Ife were creative, hardworking, and known for making great artwork and sculptures. All the men in her town, including married men, wished to marry Moremi. She ended up married to King Oranmiyan and thus became the queen of the ancient Yoruba city-state of Ile-Ife.

Together, they had a son named Oluorogbo. At the time, the Yoruba town of Ile-Ife was subjected to frequent invasions by the forest people who lived nearby. They robbed the Ife market on a regular basis, stealing properties, staple foods, and domestic animals. Hundreds of Yoruba were also captured as slaves by these forest people, who had such strange appearances on the battlefield that the Yorubas mistook them for evil spirits. Many believed they were visitations sent by the gods as punishment for some evil deeds they had committed.

The repeated raids put the people of Ile-Ife in continual terror for their lives. Queen Moremi saw the devastation of her people and, in her virtue, decided that she could no longer let that continue. She made up her mind that she was going to put an end to this horrifying situation.

Upon devising a strategy, Moremi paid a visit to the spirit of the River Esimirin, promising to make the greatest sacrifice conceivable if she could uncover the secret behind the forest people's strength. Her life would be forever changed as a result of this decision. And so it happened that, one fateful day, during one of their occasional raids, disguised as a mere trader, she allowed herself to be captured so that

ILLUSTRATED BY
BABA AMINU MUSTAPHA

she might be taken to the forest people's territory and learn all their secrets. Taken to the neighboring tribe, Moremi, along with the other captives, was paraded before the ruler. She was of such great beauty that as soon as the king of the forest people set eyes on her, he fell helplessly in love with her and quickly made her his new queen.

Over time, the king became so charmed by her beauty that he began to reveal to her the tricks and secrets behind these strange creatures that invaded Ile-Ife. It was then that she realized that these weird creatures were humans disguised as masquerades, dressed in dried grasses and bamboo fibers to terrorize their enemies. She also discovered that they were terrified of fire and that if the Yoruba people attacked them with lighted torches, they would be easily defeated.

As soon as she could, she planned her escape back to her homeland, Ile-Ife, and eventually succeeded. All that Queen Moremi had learned was relayed to her people. As a result, the next time these weird creatures came to attack the Yorubas, they were driven away by burning torches. This eventually put an end to the frequent raids. After her victory, Queen Moremi returned to her first husband, who was glad to reinstate her as his queen. She then went back to the Esimirin River to fulfill her oath. The Esimirin deity demanded she sacrifice her only son. Devastated, she pleaded for a less horrific offering, to no avail. Though deeply saddened by the request, Moremi finally kept her oath and surrendered her only son.

The sacrifice of her son deeply grieved Queen Moremi and the entire kingdom of Ife. She was consoled by the Yoruba people, who wept bitterly with her and promised to be her eternal children.

The Edi Festival celebrated to this day, in which people dress up in raffias and are chased around by torchbearers, was founded to honor her bravery and enormous sacrifice.

To this date, the Yoruba people continue to grieve with her and hold her in the highest regard of all the women in the entire kingdom.

QUEEN ABLA POKOU
(1700 - 1760)

Once upon a time, there lived a princess called Abla Pokou. Following the death of the powerful Osei Tutu, king of the Ashanti Empire, a succession conflict erupted, and Dakon, Abla Pokou's brother, one of the heirs to the throne, was killed. Fearing for her life and family, Abla Pokou gathered a large caravan and escaped, leading her people westward toward the Comoé River. During their escape, they made their way through endless jungles, where they had to fight panthers, big ants, and giant snakes. They passed through savannas filled with ferocious elephants and serpents that appeared to be waiting for them no matter where they went.

After many months of running away, Princess Pokou and her followers finally reached the banks of the Comoé River and could go no further. Because of the persistent rain, the river was at its highest level, making it impossible to cross. Princess Abla Pokou consulted the wise men who accompanied them and was told that the river gods demanded a sacrifice in the form of a child from a noble bloodline for them to cross the river. Heartbroken, Abla Pokou had no other choice than to throw her child into the river to save her people as the enemy troops were getting closer. Her son vanished into the swells. As soon as that happened, enormous hippopotamuses and crocodiles appeared, lining up to form a pathway over the river for Abla Pokou and her followers to cross.

After the crossing, all the animals disappeared, making it impossible for their enemies to reach them. On their new land, Princess Abla Pokou established the Baoule nation, which is known today as the Ivory Coast. Today, she is still referred to as the mother of the Ivory Coast.

ILLUSTRATED BY
NILS KWASI BRITWUM

QUEEN IDIA

(15TH TO 16TH CENTURY)

Once upon a time, there was a little girl who loved dancing. As she grew up, her dancing skills became even better. During one of the capital's dance performances, Idia danced so well that she caught the attention of King (Oba) Ozolua. When the oba expressed interest in her, her parents did everything they could to prevent him from marrying their daughter.

This is because, once married to the oba, a lady was forbidden to see her immediate family. Unfortunately, their attempts failed, and Idia eventually married Oba Ozulua. According to tradition, women were only expected to serve their husbands, care for their children, and handle other domestic matters. This role, however, changed over time, thanks to Queen Idia.

Queen Idia maneuvered her son Osawe's (Oba Esigie) way to the throne and later served as his advisor throughout his reign, occasionally fighting alongside him whenever necessary. She became the first woman to be given a first-class chieftaincy title. She was the first and best female warrior in the Benin kingdom, and she led the Benin armies in several successful wars. She raised her own army and defeated her son's enemies using ancient medicine and magic.

Queen Idia brought significant changes to the empire's political, cultural, and social laws. Today, the people of Edo look to Queen Idia as a role model and heroine. Following Idia, other women began accompanying their husbands to battlefields.

To this day, Queen Mother Idia's facemask is the most well-known face of an African royal woman after that of the Egyptian queen Nefertiti.

ILLUSTRATED BY
BABA AMINU MUSTAPHA

QUEEN LILIUOKALANI
(1838 - 1917)

Once upon a time, there was a smart and talented little girl called Liliuokalani. Liliuokalani had a very beautiful voice, she loved to sing, and she never wasted an opportunity to write a new song. Being of noble origin, young Liliuokalani paid frequent visits to the Western world, as was customary for young members of the Hawaiian nobility in those days.

In 1862, she got married to John Owen Dominusi. Liliuokalani's elder brother, David Kalākaua, would later be appointed king. During his reign, King Kalākaua would go on a world tour and would have Liliuokalani act as a regent during his absence. Later, when King Kalākaua died, Liliuokalani ascended to the throne, becoming Hawaii's first female ruler. As queen, she built numerous schools and worked to put in place a new constitution that would restore the monarchy's rights, which had previously been lost.

Throughout her rule, Liliuokalani protested fiercely against the United States' annexation of the Hawaiian Islands. However, annexation eventually took place in July 1898. In the same year, she released "Hawaii's Story by Hawaii's Queen" and wrote "Aloha Oe," a song that has been popular on the islands ever since. She retired from public life after that, receiving a government pension and the respect of both islanders and visitors. She is best recognized for her work to empower women, her fight for the Hawaiian monarchy, and her status as Hawaii's first and only black queen.

She is also famous for being a talented musician who wrote over 160 songs and chants throughout her lifetime, including "Aloha Oe," which has become one of the most popular songs in Hawaiian history.

ILLUSTRATED BY
MIRACLE UZOMEFUNA

QUEEN YODIT GUDIT

(10TH CENTURY AD)

Once upon a time, there lived a young and beautiful rebel princess called Gudit. Princess Gudit was a brave and daring young lady who would go to any length to achieve her goals. This little princess later rose through the ranks to become the first queen of Zagwe.

Queen Gudit waged war on the very powerful kingdom of Axum, conquered it, took the throne, and reigned for forty years. During her reign, she maintained good relations with other countries, established a completely new dynasty, and expanded Ethiopia's borders further west and south.

She is remembered today as a legendary warrior queen who led a horse-mounted army of men. She is also labeled Ethiopia's most fearsome warrior, having destroyed the Axum Empire and seized the throne by force. Thanks to her bravery, her people named her Esato, which means **"fire."**

ILLUSTRATED BY
BABA AMINU MUSTAPHA

QUEEN MUHUMUZA
(UNKNOWN - 1945)

A hundred years ago, a queen named Muhumuza battled imperialism in Uganda and Rwanda. She was described by most as having an extraordinary character and was one of the most formidable queens that ever lived.

Queen Muhumuza led a movement known as the Nyabingi movement, a religious movement that promoted the belief in a female deity as the source of fertility, health, and farm harvests. Following the death of King Rwabugiri in 1895, a succession battle ensued, prompting Queen Muhumuza and her son Biregeya to flee north to avoid a massacre. While in the north, Muhumuza claimed authority with the assistance of the Abakiga people of Southern Uganda. Her fame grew, and she eventually became the most feared female rebel, leading an anticolonial uprising that promised to drive British and German colonialists out of her country.

Queen Muhumuza would have six men carry her shoulder-high on a palanquin whenever she needed to travel. She also had a fortified home surrounded by up to three thousand people. Queen Muhumuza's movement has left a lasting legacy in her country and beyond.

She is remembered today as a charismatic spiritual and military leader who fought for justice and promoted women's rights in society.

ILLUSTRATED BY
BABA AMINU MUSTAPHA

PRINCESS YENNENGA
(11TH and 15TH CENTURIES)

Once upon a time, there was a princess called Yennenga who lived in a faraway kingdom. Princess Yennenga was seen as the most beautiful woman in the entire Dagomba kingdom. No one could compete with her father's love for her. King Nedega admired his daughter not just for her unrivaled beauty but also for her skill with the sword and spear, as well as her ability to ride and tame even the most powerful stallions. Her bravery and strength rivaled that of his strongest warriors.

Princess Yennenga was widely loved and adored. She went to war with her father against the neighboring Malinke people when she was only fourteen years old. She was an exceptional horsewoman who rode better than her brothers and the warriors of the kingdom. Her most powerful weapons were javelins, spears, and arrows, which she wielded in battles as if she were a man. Everyone praised her for her bravery, and she was highly honored amongst her people, as it was not customary for a woman in those days to go to war.

Despite being praised as one of the greatest warriors of the Dagomba, Princess Yennenga was often afflicted with sadness. As she grew older, she greatly desired to find her prince, an idea which her father greatly disliked. On many occasions, she begged her father to give her away in marriage, but he refused. It was inconceivable for him to even think of losing his greatest warrior to marriage. Her father's opposition to her wish to marry saddened her greatly. One day, an idea came to her. Taking matters into her own hands, she decided to plant a vast field of wheat. Her father was so taken aback by the gorgeous wheat field that he boasted about her agricultural exploits to all his elite acquaintances.

ILLUSTRATED BY
Tosin Akinwande

After a few months, she let the wheat decay. Her father was surprised and inquired as to why she did that. This was Princess Yennenga's reply: "You see, Father, as precious as you say I am, you still let me rot like the wheat in this field."

Furious with anger, King Nedega imprisoned her in the palace. And that is how days became weeks and weeks became months. Princess Yennenga was fortunate enough to have friends among the king's guards, as she was very well loved. As a result, one of the king's guards assisted Princess Yennenga in escaping. He dressed her up as a man and presented her with her stallion. Both rode late into the night, their minds centered on thoughts of freedom. Unfortunately, they were eventually spotted and attacked by Malinke warriors.

The king's guard knew it was impossible for both to survive should they decide to fight together. So, with all his strength, he fought the Malinke soldiers by himself, and one by one, they fell at his feet. Sadly, his efforts were not enough, and he was killed. However, his heroic effort distracted their attention away from Princess Yennenga, who was able to flee. Deeply saddened, and now alone deep in the forest, far away from her people, she decided to be brave and carry on northward. At one point, she had to cross a torrid river. And being the fearless woman she was, she skillfully navigated the powerful currents and successfully got to the other side of the river.

Princess Yennenga was exhausted from her efforts and slept on the back of her horse, but suddenly she noticed a house. It belonged to Riale, a famous elephant hunter.

When Riale first saw Yennenga, he quickly bowed, mistaking her for a Malinke warrior because she was dressed so elegantly in men's clothing. Riale let Yennenga stay in his home. After some time, she realized he was a good man and decided to reveal to him who she was.

"I am Princess Yennenga, daughter of Nedegar, princess of the Dagomba." Following this revelation, the two fell in love, and Princess Yennenga later gave birth to a boy named Ouedraogo, which means "stallion."

Over time, Princess Yennenga reconciled with her father. Ouedraogo became the founder of the powerful Mossi kingdom. The legendary princess Yennenga is said to be the mother of the Mossi people of modern-day Burkina Faso.

PRINCESS NANDI

(1760s - 1827)

Once upon a time, a woman named Nandi had a forbidden relationship with Senzangakhona, the chief of the Zulu tribe. From this relationship a son was born named Shaka Zulu. When Nandi first informed King Senzangakhona of her pregnancy, he initially denied the child as his, but later decided to marry her due to pressure.

Once married, she was treated as a lowly third wife and suffered a lot of bullying from Senzangakhona's other wives and their children. Over time, the pain grew to be too much for Nandi to bear, so she decided to run away with Shaka. Together, they wandered about until they met with the Mthethwa clan, who welcomed them. The clan leader, Diniswago, loved Shaka dearly and taught him how to lead and fight. They stayed with the Mthethwa clan until Shaka returned to the Zulu people and forcefully seized the throne. Once Shaka became king, he appointed Nandi as queen of the Zulu people and his advisor.

Queen Nandi had great influence over the affairs of the kingdom. She was the voice of reason during times of political conflict with neighboring kingdoms. Thanks to her support, King Shaka was able to greatly expand his kingdom.

Queen Nandi's story is a remarkable one about a mother's love. She suffered great humiliation from almost everybody but remained devoted to raising her son the best she could. Her son, Shaka, would end up being one of the greatest warriors and African military leaders of all time.

ILLUSTRATED BY
Tosin Akinwande

QUEEN AMANIRENAS
(60 OR 50BC -10BC)

Once upon a time, there was a kingdom known as the kingdom of Kush. Their land was referred to as the Land of the Bows. This was because the Nubian hunters and warriors, both women and men, were excellent archers. Queen Amanirenas was the most famous of them all. During her reign, emperor Caesar Augustus of the Roman Empire defeated the Egyptians and desired to further expand his province, into the kingdom of Kush. Determined to stop the Roman invasion, Queen Amanirenas led an army of thirty thousand soldiers to fight the Romans in Egypt.

Queen Amanirenas led the front of her army, fighting alongside her men. She launched a surprise attack, which was a huge success. She was able to capture three major Roman cities, took prisoners, and destroy countless sculptures of Emperor Ceasar. To show her hatred for the emperor, she removed the head of one of his statues and buried it under the entranceway of her palace so everyone could walk over his head. Because of their large army, the Roman Empire easily took back its cities, invaded Kush, and declared victory far too soon.

Queen Amanirenas attacked back immediately, using her best war tactics to gain an advantage over her enemies. After three years of intense battle, a peace treaty highly favorable to the Nubians was signed. Emperor Caesar and the queen agreed to remove his army from Egypt, return the Kushites' land, and withdraw their forces.

Queen Amanirenas ruled the kingdom of Kush until her death in 10 BC. Today, she is remembered as a brave woman who led her kingdom to great victories.

ILLUSTRATED BY
BABA AMINU MUSTAPHA

PRINCESS MKABAYI
(1750 - 1843)

Many have heard legends about Shaka Zulu; however, few are familiar with the story of the princess who was the power behind his ascension to the throne. This is the story of a Zulu princess called Princess Mkabayi!

Once upon a time, in what is today known as South Africa, there lived a Zulu king named Jama. When Jama's wife became pregnant, the entire nation celebrated, eagerly anticipating the birth of a new male heir. The queen gave birth to twin daughters, Mkabayi and Mmama, instead of the much-anticipated boy. The birth of twins was frowned upon in Zulu tradition. The people therefore demanded that King Jama kill his twin girls, but he adored them too much and chose not to do so. As the twins got older, the Zulu people continued to despise them, blaming them for everything that went wrong within the kingdom.

The bravest of the two princesses, Mkabayi, often took most of the blame. Realizing that her father, the king, was growing old and still without a male heir, she searched for him a new bride in secret and eventually introduced him to Mthaniya Sibiya, who soon became the next queen. And finally, to the delight of the Zulu people, a male heir named Senzangakhona kajama was born from this relationship. Thanks to this achievement, Mkabayi had proven herself to be worthy of the people's respect. And so began her long influence on the Zulu kingdom's politics, which spanned the succeeding reigns of three kings.

When King Jama passed away, Princess Mkabayi assumed leadership while her brother matured into his position as the future king. She proved to be a highly capable regent at a period when having a female counselor was unheard of.

ILLUSTRATED BY
Tosin Akinwande

Although the Zulu people were doubtful of Mkabayi since she was a woman, she proved time and time again that she was an exceptional leader who always put the kingdom's unity first. She prevented assassination attempts on her brother's life and crushed other aspirations to the throne.

Mkabayi eventually stepped down when her half-brother was mature enough to rule the kingdom. Though she was no longer the regent, she remained politically active in the Zulu kingdom, utilizing her power to influence decisions and do what she believed was best for the Zulu people. When her brother had a son out of wedlock, she intervened immediately, encouraging the mother to escape with her son before they could be captured. Nandi was the woman's name, and Shaka was her son.

When Senzangakhona died, Mkabayi assisted his son, Shaka Zulu, in successfully assuming the throne. Under Shaka's leadership, the Zulu kingdom prospered and expanded tremendously. After Shaka's mother died, grief caused Shaka to institute irrational laws that caused great harm to the Zulu people. Wishing to preserve the Zulu kingdom, Mkabayi conspired to get him replaced, a plot that worked, as Shaka was successfully replaced by Dingane.

During the reign of Dingane, Mkabayi would continue to serve as a great advisor as she had done under the reigns of Shaka and Senzangakhona.

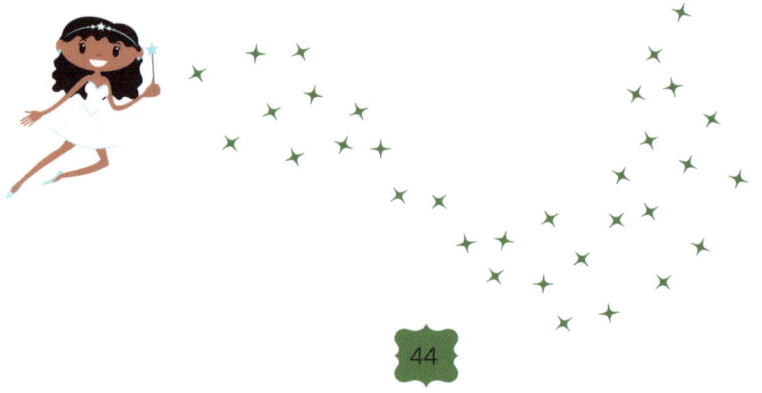

She repeatedly turned away suitors who desired her hand in marriage, dedicating her entire life to serving the growing Zulu kingdom. Thanks to her sacrifice, the Zulu empire grew to become one of the greatest empires in history.

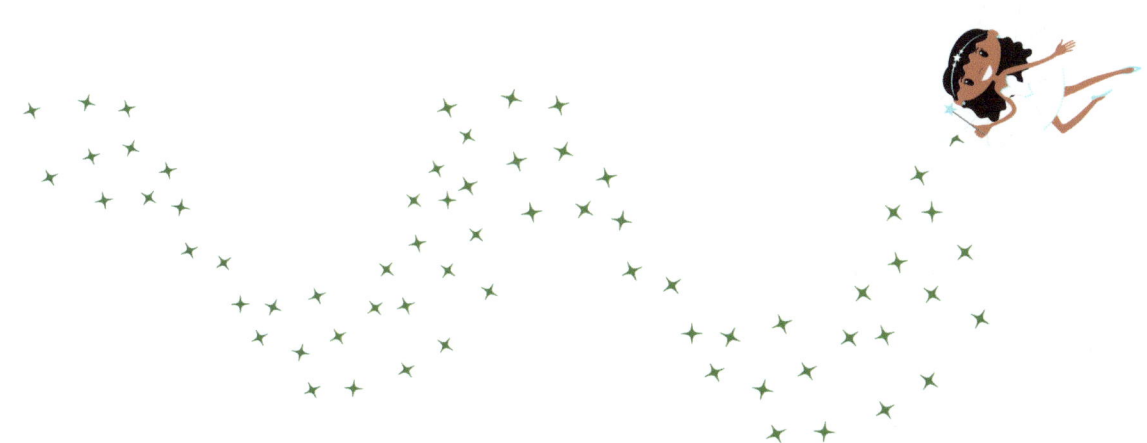

QUEEN RANAVALONA
(1778 - 1861)

Once upon a time, there was a little girl who lived on a beautiful island. Little Ranavalona was not of noble background but had been adopted into the royal family as a reward for her father's courageous act of exposing a murder plot against the king. Later, King Andrianampoinimerina passed away and was succeeded by Prince Radama, who got married to Ranavalona. King Radama followed in his father's footsteps and allowed foreign invasions of the island, a notion that highly displeased the queen.

In 1828, King Radama also passed away and was to be replaced by his nephew, Prince Rakatobe. As soon as this plan of succession came to the knowledge of Ranavalona, she gathered supporters to bring down their plan and any other potential regent to the crown. Her plan worked, and in 1829, she declared herself queen of Madagascar.

Completely against the European invasion, Queen Ranavalona's next move was to change the reforms implemented by her husband. She reformed society to return to her people's traditional customs and values. European businessmen, instructors, and diplomats were banished, and commercial agreements with Britain and France were completely annulled. After a victorious battle against an invasion, she lined up the defeated European soldiers on the beaches of her island with the intention of scaring away any further foreign invasions.

Most consider Queen Ranavalona to have been a tyrannical leader, while others admire her patriotic and tactical leadership in preserving Madagascar's independence, something her predecessors had failed to do.

ILLUSTRATED BY
TOSIN AKINWANDE

QUEEN NEFERTITI
(c. 1370- c. 1330 BC)

Once upon a time, there was a lovely little girl named Nefertiti, whose name meant "a beautiful woman has come." Nefertiti was indeed beautiful and well loved by many. At about fifteen years of age, Nefertiti got married to King Akhenaten.

Together, they took an active role in establishing the Aten cult, a religious mythology that established Aten, the sun, as the most important god in Egypt's polytheistic canon. Nefertiti and King Akhenaten also promoted a style of Egyptian art that was entirely different from that of their predecessors.

Today, she is remembered for her extreme beauty as well as her religious revolution alongside her husband.

ILLUSTRATED BY
BABA AMINU MUSTAPHA

PRIESTESS NEHANDA
(c.1840- c. 1898)

Once upon a time, there lived a girl named Nehanda. Growing up, she witnessed the injustice committed by the British settlers in her land. Led by a desire to establish justice, Nehanda began to rally her people all over the land, encouraging them to arm themselves for battle. Her words were always well heard, as she had an eloquence of speech that always gave hope to the people around her. Nehanda was a great leader.

She organized meetings, gave great speeches, and armed her soldiers with tactical war strategies to use during battles so they would defeat their enemies. Over time, she became both a military and political as well as a spiritual leader for the people of Mashonaland. At her command, they fought for their independence.

Today, Priestess Nehanda is remembered as a lady of very strong principles and character who fought against the British invasion of Zimbabwe. She dedicated her life to fighting for and with her people against colonization. Her desire was to see her people live in peace and harmony and be in charge of their destiny.

Today, she is a heroine and a true nationalist figure for the people of Zimbabwe.

ILLUSTRATED BY
BABA AMINU MUSTAPHA

EMPRESS MARIE CLAIRE BOHNEUR

(1758 - 1858)

Once upon a time, there was a little girl called Marie-Claire. Marie-Claire was born to a poor family. Despite her poverty, she was the kindest little girl you could ever meet. Growing up, Marie-Claire loved caring for the sick and providing for the needy, a skill which proved to be of much help during the fight for Haiti's independence. During the war, she managed to convince Jean-Jacques Dessalines, one of the leaders whose forces surrounded the city, to keep the roads open so she could take care of the wounded.

She also gathered a good number of women and girls whom she convinced to join her in distributing food, clothes, and medicine to the wounded soldiers. Thanks to her actions, Marie-Claire was later qualified as the first war nurse in the history of Haiti. She went as far as mounting wounded soldiers on her horse and taking them to her home so she could administer them with better treatments. Completely falling under her charm because of her caring, compassionate, elegant, and gentle nature, Jean-Jacques Dessalines courted her for a while, and the two eventually got married.

When Haiti's monarchy was established, she was named Empress Marie-Claire and crowned alongside her husband on October 8, 1804. They had a total of seven children. After Dessalines passed away, with all his properties confiscated, she moved in with her granddaughter, with whom she lived until the end of her days.

In memory of her generosity, the Fondation Marie-Claire Heureuse Félicité Bonheur Dessalines was founded in 1999 to handle humanitarian and educational activities in Haiti.

ILLUSTRATED BY
KIARA NAYBAB

QUEEN OF SHEBA (MAKEDA)

(10TH CENTURY BC)

Once upon a time, there lived a queen of great wealth and beauty called Makeda. This mighty queen ruled over the kingdom of Axum. One day, Tamrin, one of Queen Makeda's merchants, upon returning from a long trip from Jerusalem, informed her about the greatness, generosity, and wisdom of the king of Israel named Solomon.

Intrigued by the great wisdom and glamour her merchant told her about, Queen Makeda took the road to Jerusalem. She left with a large group of attendants and camels, taking with her loads of spices, jewels, precious stones, and large amounts of gold. She intended to present these as gifts to King Solomon. After a couple of years' journey, Queen Makeda finally arrived in Jerusalem and was warmly welcomed. As desired, she met with King Solomon and asked him all the hard questions she had prepared for him, intending to test his knowledge.

To her satisfaction, he answered them all, which left her astounded. Not only was she mesmerized by the wisdom of King Solomon, but she was also highly impressed by all the wealth he possessed as well as his relationship with his almighty God. Convinced, she converted to King Solomon's religion. With each passing day spent at the palace, both Queen Makeda and King Solomon became fond of each other, leading to a brief love affaire. Then came the time for Queen Makeda to return to her people. Before she could leave, King Solomon gave her a ring as a token of his faith.

On her way home, she gave birth to a son and called him Menilek, meaning "son of a wise man." Menelik would grow up to become the first Solomonic emperor of Ethiopia.

ILLUSTRATED BY
Tosin Akinwande

PRINCESS AQUALTUNE
(UNKNOWN -1675)

Once upon a time, there was a beautiful princess called Aqualtune. Princess Aqualtune was a courageous young girl who could not stand still in the face of injustice.

She despised the ways of the Portuguese in her land and was determined to do something about it. In 1655, she decided to lead a large number of ten thousand men and women into the Battle of Mbwila.

Today, she is remembered as a woman of undeniable strength and a fighter for justice.

ILLUSTRATED BY
MIRACLE UZOMEFUNA

PRIESTESS KIMPA VITA
(1684 - 1706)

Once upon a time, there was a girl named Kimpa Vita. She was a very spiritual little girl who would grow up to become an influential religious leader of the Kongo Empire. Growing up, Kimpa Vita frequently received visions and messages from the heavens. Because of these visions, in her later years, she created her own Christian movement, known as the Antonian Movement.

The Antonian Movement, also known as African Christianity, was a mix of Christianity and African religious practices. This movement had the objective of recognizing black saints. Within a very short time, Kimpa Vita was able to gather a good number of followers and send missionaries of her movement to other cities. She warned the leaders of Kongo not to let the Portuguese in, as their intentions were not all that pure, though they remained hidden under the umbrella of the church.

Her prophecy eventually came to pass as the Portuguese settled in and began their slave trade activities. Kimpa Vita gathered a large number of followers and became a leader in the Kongo Empire's struggle for independence. She was determined to save her people from the hands of the Portuguese and from their deformed doctrines.

Today, Kimpa Vita is remembered as the mother of African unity.

ILLUSTRATED BY
TAIYE OKOH

EMPRESS TAYTU
(1851 - 1918)

Once upon a time, there lived a little brave girl called Taytu. Little Taytu was born into a Christian and Muslim family in Wollo. After four unsuccessful marriages, Taytu's last marriage was to Emperor Menelik II. Their marriage was about independence and cooperation, marked by trust, respect, and reciprocity. She was his equal, and he always sought her advice before making important decisions. Determined to resist imperialist aspirations for her country, Empress Taytu bravely rejected any agreements that would result in the loss of the Ethiopian territory. When battle was unavoidable, she rode out at the head of her own army, by her husband's side.

Empress Taytu also organized women, both as fighters and nurses of wounded soldiers. She was the first to persuade Emperor Menelek II and other men to stand up for independence against Italian aggression by declaring war on Italy. As a military strategist, she devised a strategy that aided Italy's defeat at the Battle of Adwa in 1896, giving the Ethiopians the most significant victory of any African army at the peak of European colonialism.

Empress Taytu Betul was a real Ethiopian leader. Her actions at a critical moment in Ethiopian history not only spared the country from European colonization but also laid the foundations for Africa's liberation.

She founded Addis Ababa, Ethiopia's capital city today, and during her rule, Ethiopia saw a period of modernization that progressively opened the country up to trade and increased technical expertise.

ILLUSTRATED BY
BABA AMINU MUSTAPHA

QUEEN NDATE YALLA
(1810 - 1860)

Once upon a time, there lived a little girl called Ndate Yalla. From a very young age, Ndate Yalla inherited the great elegance and courage of her ancestors. As a little girl, she was so well behaved and always carried herself with the pride and authority typical of a dignified queen. As she grew up, Ndate Yalla succeeded to the throne of the Waalo kingdom at the age of thirty-six following the death of her sister.

Once she became queen, she ruled the kingdom with an iron hand, representing a real threat to the French colonists who had settled in Senegal. At their first encounter with the queen, the French forces were shocked to witness a tenacious resistance led by a woman. This was very uncommon to them, as women were not recognized as citizens in France until a couple of decades later. The French soldiers were surprised by this beautiful and proud woman of great elegance who led an enormous army.

Queen Ndate Yalla organized a strong women's army, which became one of the most formidable forces against colonialism. She fought both the Moors and the colonialist forces, who wanted to take over her land. In the years following her reign, she continued to defy French colonialism and the invasion of the Moors, fighting countless battles to maintain the independence of her kingdom. This resistance lasted until the early twentieth century. The lingeer (queen) Ndate Yalla Mbodj was the last great queen of the Waalo kingdom, located in the northwest of modern-day Senegal.

Today, she is remembered as a hero of colonial resistance and has remained a symbol of female empowerment.

ILLUSTRATED BY
BABA AMINU MUSTAPHA

QUEEN DIHYA
(7TH CENTURY)

Once upon a time, there was a tall, fearless, and determined princess named Dihya. Princess Dihya was the daughter of Berber king Aksel, a well-known freedom fighter. Young Princess Dihya had two little secrets nobody knew. Her first secret was her ability to foretell the future, and her second secret was her ability to communicate with birds. Because of her superpowers, she was nicknamed "al-Kahina," which translates to "priestess soothsayer."

Following the death of King Altava of Kusaila, Princess Dihya took over the throne and became queen. Her reign lasted for five years. During these years, she established herself as a great military strategist. She formed and led a strong resistance against the Arabs who invaded her homeland on a regular basis. She eventually became the queen of most of the Berbers of Northern Africa.

Today, Queen Dihya is remembered as a military and religious leader who led a resistance against the Arab extension of northwest Africa, which is today's modern-day Algeria.

ILLUSTRATED BY
BABA AMINU MUSTAPHA

QUEEN CALIFIA

(UNKNOWN)

Once upon a time, in a far-off land, almost completely hidden from humanity, there lived a golden decorated warrior general called Queen Califia. Little Califia was not like any other young girl out there. She had a superpower: she could communicate with animals. Over time, she developed a series of animal training techniques that proved to be useful, as these trained animals became excellent war allies.

As the years went by, Califia took over power of her land and became the reigning queen. She was a grand and beautiful royal leader of a land full of gold, diamonds, rare birds, food, and precious stones. Queen Califia was also a great military strategist who commanded a vast group of ships. During her reign, she raised an army of women warriors whom she trained to become undefeatable.

These brave Amazons had beautiful, robust bodies with armors made of gold and always fought alongside trained war animals. Today, Queen Califia is often portrayed as the spirit of California and is believed to have been an important figure in California's origin.

One of the most famous paintings of her alongside her Amazons can be found in the Room of the Dons at the Mark Hopkins Hotel, San Francisco, California.

ILLUSTRATED BY
Miracle Uzomefuna

QUEEN CLEOPATRA

(69BC - 30BC)

Once upon a time, there was a very beautiful and intelligent young girl named Cleopatra. Upon the death of her father, at age eighteen, Cleopatra inherited the throne alongside her brother Ptolemy XIII. Because of their eight years age difference, Cleopatra acted as the dominant ruler. Ptolemy XIII, clearly dissatisfied with his sister's seniority, decided to drive her out of power with the help of his followers, causing her to flee to Syria.

After raising an entire army, Cleopatra returned to Egypt. With the help of ancient Rome's leader, Julius Caesar, she reclaimed the throne as a co-ruler alongside her brother Ptolemy XIV. Shortly after, Ptolemy XIV died, leaving Cleopatra and her son as the sole rulers of Egypt.

Today, Cleopatra is remembered as an extremely beautiful and attractive queen who had a significant influence on Roman politics and helped build the Egyptian economy. She was the last ruler of the Macedonian dynasty in Egypt.

ILLUSTRATED BY
MIRACLE UZOMEFUNA

RAIN QUEENS OF SOUTH AFRICA

(UNKNOWN)

Once upon a time, in a faraway kingdom known as the Monomotapa, there lived a princess called Princess Dzugundini. A great sin was committed in the kingdom of Monomotapa, a sin so great that the people had to demand the death of the princess to purge the sin of their land. Seeing that his daughter's life was in danger, King Mugodo intervened and gave his daughter rainmaking powers, telling her to head south into South Africa. Heartbroken and having to flee her land like a thief, the young princess escaped south, where she formed her own kingdom and named it Balodedu.

There, a strict matrilineal system was born for the Balobedu people, producing a line of royal rain queens whereby only the firstborn female could inherit the throne. The rain queens, known as the "Mujaji," had the power to manipulate the weather and influence nature, especially the clouds and rain. The rain queens were known as extremely powerful magicians, able to bring rain to their friends and drought to their enemies.

As a result, the Mujajis were feared and respected for centuries by many. Not a single African king would want to be their enemy, fearing punishment in the form of severe drought, which usually lasted for years. Even the well-renowned king Shaka Zulu would often send his top emissaries to request the blessings of the rain queens. To reinforce their power, once a year, a ceremony was organized known as the Rain-Making Ceremony.

The rain queens were the first all-women-led royal monarchy in history. They are still alive today and can be found in the Limpopo province of South Africa.

ILLUSTRATED BY
Taiye Okoh

SEH-DONG-HONG-BEH
(UNKNOWN)

Once upon a time, there lived a lovely and beautiful little girl called Seh-Dong-Hong-Beh. From a very young age, she aspired to become an Amazon. Seh-Dong-Hong-Beh admired the strength and courage of the Dahomey Amazons and dreamed day and night of what it would be like to become one of them, so she trained as hard as she could. At only ten years of age, she exhibited so much strength and courage that she was eventually chosen to train as an Amazon.

This was such a great honor for Seh-Dong-Hong-Beh and her entire family, as those chosen to be amongst the Dahomey Amazons (Minos) benefitted from exquisite royal treatment. Seh-Dong-Hong-Beh trained even harder and distinguished herself from the others to the point where, at the age of fifteen, she was chosen to lead the all-female army that was preparing for war against the Egba of Abeokuta (an ethnic group in western Nigeria).

Thanks to her strength and intelligence, she and her group of six thousand female warriors succeeded in taking over the Egba fortress, obtaining several slaves for her kingdom. Amazed by her exploits, the king further trusted her with many other missions of such importance, in which she always proved successful. As a result, she gained a lot of royal favors from the king and his royal entourage. Seh-Dong-Hong-Beh had special apartments in the king's palace and had servants to cater to her every need.

Today, she is remembered as being a woman of undeniable strength and courage who did not fear to lead her army to countless victories. She is proof that women are worth much more.

ILLUSTRATED BY
Taiye Okoh

DAHOMEY AMAZONS

(UNKNOWN -1904)

Once upon a time, in a kingdom known as Dahomey, there lived a king called King Ghezo. During his reign, King Ghezo decided to create an all-female military group, later known as the Dahomey Amazons. Members of this group of Amazon female fighters were referred to as the Mino, or Mothers, and oversaw the protection of the kingdom of Dahomey from its enemies.

These Dahomey Amazons devoted their lives to battle and vowed never to bear children. Maintaining the peace of the Dahomey and the sovereignty of their king was their only objective. The Mino female fighters had to go through rigorous physical training. During their training, they learned survival skills and discipline and were taught to be indifferent to pain. Women were able to ascend to assume positions of authority and influence while serving in the Mino.

The Minos were considered to be women of great wealth and were held in high status amongst all the Dahomey people. Divided into several military formations, the Amazons included huntresses, riflewomen, reapers, archers, and gunners, who carried their own massive iron weapons. Each military formation also had its own female commanders, uniforms, weapons, and traditions.

The Dahomey Amazons were praised by all, even by their enemies. They were outstandingly brave, well trained for combat, and never scared to go into war. Their legacy remains with us forever. Today, the Amazons are regarded as a symbol of female emancipation.

ILLUSTRATED BY
Tosin Akinwande

QUEEN HATSHEPSUT

(1508BC - 1458BC)

Once upon a time, there lived a little girl called Hatshepsut. Hatshepsut was the daughter of King Thutmose I. She was a brave, spirited, and ambitious young lady. Thanks to her courage and determination, growing up, she was able to ascend to the throne and became the second female pharaoh of ancient Egypt and the first to attain the full power of her title as pharaoh.

Queen Hatshepsut promoted trade between Egypt and other countries. She is known to have launched a very successful trading expedition to a faraway land known as Punt, bringing back great riches to Egypt in the form of gold, ivory, incense, and leopard skin.

Hatshepsut is also remembered today as one of the greatest builders in ancient Egypt.

ILLUSTRATED BY
Tosin Akinwande

QUEEN YAA ASANTEWAA
(1840 - 1921)

This is the story of Queen Yaa Asantewaa, the strongest female figure of the Ashanti Empire.

On the west coast of the motherland lived a large group of people called the Ashanti. The Ashantis were very good artisans and goldsmiths. They used a lot of gold, since it was abundant in the land. It was very common for the women and children to wear gold ornaments from head to toe, complementing their vibrant outfits. In the olden days, the Ashanti people were scattered across the land in small clans ruled by chiefs.

This was so until the great Osei Tutu felt the burden of uniting all the Ashanti people into one kingdom. He was successful in uniting his people and, as a result, became the first king of the Ashanti kingdom and sole guardian of the golden stool. The golden stool was a unique, beautifully designed stool said to have fallen from the sky. It was bright and shiny, the most wonderful piece of furniture anyone had ever seen. It was made largely of gold and had wonderful engravings that could only suggest divine craftsmanship.

The stool came with very firm instructions. It had to be kept hidden, and the king's bottom could touch it only three times and only during a ceremony called The Installment. The golden stool represented the true spirit of the Ashanti people, and if they followed all the instructions given along with the stool, their bond would be strengthened, and they would remain united forever. The great Osei Tutu, very pleased with the gift from the sky, did everything that had been instructed. From generation to generation, the stool remained amongst the Ashanti, and, indeed, their bond grew stronger over time, with the empire witnessing many years of peace and prosperity until the arrival of the British invaders.

ILLUSTRATED BY
NILS KWASI BRITWUM

They came because of their interest in all the gold in the Ashanti soil and were resisted fiercely, causing a lot of unrest in the Ashanti kingdom for a long time. Finally, in the early 1900s, the British decided to get a hold of the Ashantis' precious golden stool, believing taking it from them would weaken their spirit and destabilize their resistance. Plus, its weight in gold alone was worth all the struggles. The British governor therefore went to the clan's chief to forcefully seize the golden stool, claiming it was the property of the queen of England. His greed went as far as demanding to sit on the stool, a request that greatly outraged the Ashanti people.

Though greatly enraged by the request, most chiefs were afraid to contradict the British governor, and with their king in exile, most of them were confused as to what to do. Nevertheless, not all were scared; among them stood a woman whose bravery was unmatchable. She was known as Queen Mother Yaa Asantewaa. She was a woman like no other. Very annoyed with the prudent attitude of the Ashanti leaders in the meeting, Queen Mother Yaa Asantewaa decided to act. Later that day, she assembled everybody promptly and gave them one of the most inspiring speeches in history. These are her exact words:

Now I have seen that some of you fear to go forward to fight for our king. If it were in the brave days of Osei Tutu, Okomfo Anokye, and Opoku Ware, leaders would not sit down to see their king taken away without firing a shot. No white man could have dared to speak to a leader of the Ashanti in the way the governor spoke to you this morning. Is it true that the bravery of the Ashanti is no more? I cannot believe it. It cannot be! I must say this: if you, the men of Ashanti, will not go forward, then we will. The women will. I shall call upon my fellow women. We will fight the white men. We will fight till the last of us falls on the battlefields
(Queen Mother Nana Yaa Asantewa, www.blackhistorybuff.com).

Her brave words restored the men's hope, pride, and dignity. And in unity, they planned to attack the British soldiers. Queen Mother Yaa Asantewaa fired the first retaliatory shot, boosting the troops' confidence from the start. At her shot, thousands ran forward and fought for the kingdom, for the future, for a new beginning, and for the Ashanti spirit, The Golden Stool. They fought for about six months, trying to protect their beloved golden stool. In the end, the British won this legendary battle known as The War of the Golden Stool, and the Ashanti people gave them the golden stool. That was, at least, how it appeared.

You see, once she realized that her people were losing to the British Army, Queen Mother Yaa Asantewaa had the best artisans create a stool that looked exactly like the original one. It was so well made that the British Army did not realize they had been deceived. Meanwhile, the Ashanti buried the real stool in a neighboring forest. Even though the empire eventually fell under British control, the Ashanti never let go of their golden stool, the source of their unified spirit, a spirit that has carried them through and kept their culture alive over the ages.

The memory of Queen Mother Yaa Asantewaa's bravery and tenacity in preserving the golden stool is still remembered and celebrated among her people to this day.

QUEEN MWANA MKISI

(UNKNOWN)

Once upon a time, there was a brave young lady named Mwana Mkisi who grew up to become a very honorable and respectable queen. On Mombasa Island, Queen Mwana Mkisi established Kongowea, a Swahili city-state, which she transformed into the first urban civilization.

Mwana Mkisi is remembered today as the mother of the twelve Swahili tribes of Mombasa, which are located in modern-day Kenya.

ILLUSTRATED BY
TAIYE OKOH

QUEEN METE LÉLÉ GEORGETTE: MY FAVORITE QUEEN

(1972 - 2021)

Once upon a time, there lived a very beautiful little girl called Georgette. Born after a hard labor, Georgette would never see her mother, as she passed away only hours after giving birth. Georgette was a very beautiful baby, and because of that, many tried to adopt her from the hospital, as was the procedure in those days when a parent was unable to pay off the maternity hospital bills.

In the end, Georgette's father sold all he had and was able to return home with his lovely daughter, who was happy to join her three other siblings. Living in a polygamous home, Georgette and her siblings suffered a great deal of jealousy and maltreatment from their step mothers. Many times, they went days without eating and only ate whenever there happened to be leftovers thrown on the floor. They also didn't have a comfortable bed on which to sleep. Despite all the hardships they went through, the four sisters remained united until the age of maturity when each finally found their lifelong partners and went separate ways.

At the age of eighteen, Georgette got married to a businessman with whom she had four girls and twin boys. She spent the rest of her life caring for her kids and bringing them up in the ways of the Lord. She showered them with so much love and affection that her own happiness seemed not to matter. Georgette would do the same for her husband, whom she always believed would eventually become a better man.

Many envied her, as she was extremely beautiful and always looked so young despite the passing years. She never allowed any form of hate to fill her heart, but instead always gave out love when faced with hatred. Whenever an opportunity presented itself, she fed the poor, visited the sick, and provided clothes for the needy.

As a result of her being a devoted Christian, later in her life, she experienced many supernatural encounters, which gave her the courage to push forward in life despite all its hardships. Georgette ended up leaving this world in September 2021 as a result of a brain aneurysm. Though she is no more, she is remembered by her kids as being one of the kindest souls and strongest female figures they have ever known.

This is what her daughters say about her:

The Lord has deemed it fit to take away the most beautiful flower of our garden. Its beauty and odorant were so striking that, though it is no more, its sweet fragrance will forever linger around.
—Ornella

I miss you, Mama, but I imagine you right now, waltzing and chanting with the saints in glory, looking even more beautiful than you have ever been. I cry because of the separation, but my heart is full of joy, for I know at last you are finally happy in heaven, receiving the reward for your years of servitude.
—Laura

Mama, you have put the bar so high that it's almost scary for me to think I could reach it. But I will try my best to love like you loved, to forgive as you forgave, to be as sincere and devoted as you have always been, and to serve as you taught me to.
—Duchelle & Laurince

It feels empty without you.
-Yvan & Loic

Mete Lélé Georgette was not the typical warrior queen. She did not use weapons nor spears, not even daggers to fight and conquer her enemies. And I can tell you she had many. Rather, she used love, virtue, and a strong moral attitude to defeat them all one after the other. She always believed that life's hardest challenges only happened to the toughest soldiers. And indeed, she was one of them. Today, she is remembered by all as a paragon of love and a woman of unwavering strength.

TOMORROW'S TRAILBLAZERS

Let me introduce you to these amazing trailblazers, Sam, Shi, Em, and Syn. If you would like to know more about them, then read to the end.

Sam is a strong, caring, and inspiring person. She has overcome so much in the short time she has graced our earth. Singing, dancing, reading, and a thirst for knowledge are just a few ways to describe parts of her personality. She is kind and loves to socialize. You will never meet a truer friend. She is a hopeless romantic with a music collection just as vast.

Shi is curious, active, and a bit of a jokester, and she loves fashion. She also loves to search for new things and see how far she can go. She tends to shy away and opens up to those who are true to themselves, which makes her feel comfortable. It's amazing how she has a strong sense of self and is always striving to develop personally.

Em is a kind, loving, sweet, artistic person and does all she can to please all those she loves. She can make the most amazing masterpieces out of pieces of scrap. She has a vision of what she wants and doesn't let others stand in her way. She is energetic, fun-loving, and vastly curious and never hesitates to reach a hand out to those who need it.

Sym is a force to be reckoned with. She is adventurous, strong, and willing to push herself past her breaking point, and she isn't afraid of failure. She may be young, but she is wise beyond her years. She learns quickly and reminds us that no matter how young you are, you are always ready for your next phase in life if given the opportunity.

,

FURTHER READINGS

It was a wonderful experience to conduct thorough research to combine all the information contained in this book. I learned so much, which I would love to share with the world. This book alone will not be enough to contain all the treasures I have discovered, which is why I would love to drop below more material for anyone interested in learning more about African history.

WEBSITES

kentakepage.com
afrikaiswoke.com
blackpast.org
africanfeministforum.com
blackhistoryheroes.com
face2faceafrica.com
historyofyesterday.com
afrolegends.com
@hometeamhistory

I hope you enjoyed!
ACKNOWLEDGMENTS

Those I love know that I love them, and words alone cannot express all that my heart wishes to express. Writing this book has been a beautiful and daunting process, and I can only thank God for letting me put a final full stop with tears of joy. It was a beautiful process because of the wealth of knowledge I was privileged to discover about a glorious African history of which I had no notion. It was a daunting process because, during the writing process, I lost what was dearest to me—my mother, my rock, my pillar, my best friend. I thought I wouldn't survive the pain, but then the Lord Jesus was merciful enough to grant me comfort, which made it possible for me to finish this book at last.

To my precious sister, Enoti Gaelle, and husband, Enoti Landry, I say kudos for being my number one supporters. To my bestie and sister with a heart of gold, Fongang Cedrine, I say thanks for always being there for me, and to all those who took time out of their very busy days to go through my manuscript and provide me with feedback, I say a wholesome thanks.

To my wonderful Project Investors, Christiane Latchieu, Tami Rossell, Orlando Chandler, Samantha, Shiloh, Emma, and Symphony Norton, thank you for believing in this project. Words alone cannot express all my gratitude, but again, to all of you who helped in this journey in one way or another, my dearest thanks to you.

ABOUT THE AUTHOR

O.C. Mogounn is a mother of three kids. With a bachelor's degree in universal economics, she took off to Canada in 2014 and enrolled in a second degree in human resource management at the University of Lethbridge, Canada. Despite her successful academic career, Ornella has always had a passion for one thing: storytelling. When she was a kid, she would often write short stories and draw cute faces in her notebooks to keep herself motivated whenever she went through her class lessons.

Over the years, she wrote many short stories, which were never published due to a busy life. Bedtime Tales of African Queens Who Slayed History is her first-ever published work. She is currently working on an African-inspired Fairy Tale series with the objective of creating more representation in the fairy-tale world, so every little girl will have a princess to identify with.

When she is not writing, Ornella enjoys listening to Christian gospel music, hanging around with her family, or rewatching her favorite childhood mangas' anime.

Through every form of distraction, she is always in search of inspiration to help fuel her imagination and create the best possible fairy-tale stories for the younger generation, as she believes storytelling can change the world and redefine the norms of society.

Coming soon!

BEDTIME TALES OF AFRICAN KINGS WHO SLAYED HISTORY